PUT YOUR HANDS IN

WINNER OF THE WALT WHITMAN AWARD FOR 2013

Sponsored by the Academy of American Poets, the Walt Whitman Award
is given annually to the winner of an open competition among American poets
who have not yet published a book of poems.

Judge for 2013: John Ashbery

CHRIS HOSEA

POEMS

PUT YOUR HANDS IN

LOUISIANA STATE UNIVERSITY PRESS   BATON ROUGE

Published by Louisiana State University Press
Manufactured in the United States of America
LSU Press Paperback Original

First printing

Designer: Barbara Neely Bourgoyne
Typefaces: Veneer and Trade Gothic, display; Adobe Caslon Pro, text
Printer and binder: Maple Press

The author wishes to thank the editors of the following magazines, where some of the poems
in this book were first published, sometimes in different form.

6x6: "Songs for a Country Drive"; *Alice Blue Review:* "Of Me to Love"; *Boston Review:*
"Dark, Understated Romantic Comedies"; *The Destroyer:* "The Matinee I Took Chicken
In"; *EOAGH:* "The Barn Party," "Gonna Dig Up Ozu," and "Hard Drive Scrub"; *Hose Less
Review:* "Granddaddy Old Grand Dad," "Wife Wellbutrin," "Father Work," "Choirboy
Skittles," and "Cousin Pot"; *'Pider:* "Lithe Brunette, Twenty-Five Years of Age"; *Prelude:*
"Across the Boss's Desk"; *Swerve:* "Everything Is Going To"; *Web Conjunctions:* "Brother
Oxycontin," "Friend's Girlfriend Kools," "Grandmother Snuff," "Mistress Damage," "Mother
Old Fashioned," and "Sister Chablis."

Library of Congress Cataloging-in-Publication Data

Hosea, Chris, 1973–
  [Poems. Selections]
  Put Your Hands In : poems / Chris Hosea.
    pages cm
  "LSU Press Paperback Original."
  ISBN 978-0-8071-5585-1 (pbk. : alk. paper) — ISBN 978-0-8071-5586-8 (pdf) —
ISBN 978-0-8071-5587-5 (epub) — ISBN 978-0-8071-5588-2 (mobi)
  I. Title.
  PS3608.O779A6 2014
  811'.6—dc23

                                                              2013028460

To A. B.

The dirty window gives me back my face

—PAUL BLACKBURN

CONTENTS

PUT YOUR HANDS IN

LITHE BRUNETTE, TWENTY-FIVE YEARS OF AGE

In my hand walks Kansas called
bodies mostly cloudy, white in flash.
Powders blurs skins what was once
a comfy couch. Spectacles not brittle
not funny, we're in agreement to
radiate the cell of you and me.
Crowded moving emotions on film
so the crowd nods or doesn't go, and
each bit player makes mordant comment.
What is today that was eleven hours since
horror and the blank page became
an ironic pose a thrill sportif graffiti.
Oh you know, everyone, just all of them
that weren't us. She learns to drift
the testament toward shoppers and ice.
You could be embarrassed pouring milk
in a mixed drink under a bridge,
but such is your vocation. Right on her
dancing dress you never touched too
just drown the mighty wedges, a way
to get away, drop fingertips in selected woods.

DARK, UNDERSTATED ROMANTIC COMEDIES

the limbs of another
touching them climbing
a ladder splayed
soft rungs give
under fingers
stopping on one knee
to tap your forehead
an invisible hat
there you lift a hood
there the air keeps clanging
but softly
smashing
so silently
lights that aren't really there
you roll over torn posters
the slope steep
seems like forever
another dash klieg light
struck by these things
it's always moving legs
breasts cast shade
that's warm there
above the floor's tremor
you sleep somewhere else
tonight and tomorrow
long enough
to find a mirror
and see if you
read pain in it

OF ME TO LOVE

Stumble upon me
I am lying all ready
particleboard shag rug foam
as flesh the system breaks
loud punch they give us
free they gave you bare walls
bricks call it a
loft plane for wonder
and shame smoke between
friendly eyes lean into my
belly words spat on that mic
can't amplify rattle rain
I saw you spreading
legs lies taut as you spoke
right in the patron's dark
lids so whisper to my pants
a way I will not hear

CHOOSE STUTTER BRIE

Slack troopers at Matchless
ashamed of their pride
a rise at The Boat Bar
a few cultured girls (not many, it's true)
swirled cocktails with red swizzles
careful not to look so hard
as the few figures at Diamond
made listless by the clanging air
what is this weather
an almost human thwack of shuffle-
board ping of guilt The Richardson
with Lou's mouth
tasted of old-fashioneds and Kools
the iPhone buzzed my thigh
dancing in The Library
leaning into an art student
a hand down her pants-front
autistic tongues coding Tompkins after
midnight a chestnut tree
once was a chestnut

I TOO AM GAY

In college I loved a boy
he was so beautiful
some scion in a Gainsborough
some hero out of Fournier
sixteen blond hair blue irises might
as well have been a girl
he blushed so hard when
he didn't understand
in case he'd been slighted
or found out in some way
we couldn't guess
I started beating off thinking
of him and me
going at it a lovely Brazilian
snug between us
I imagined it was okay
Bruna was in the fantasy I wasn't gay
I felt lucky Philip was my friend
my heart hurt when he left
for a western cowboy college all guys
one summer we met in Baltimore
drank a lot took bong rips
I got excited and anxious
finally I would kiss a boy's tongue a boy's lips
and what could that mean
but I held back and he
certainly wasn't the type to lead
later when at last he started snoring
I tiptoed to the bath
locked the door
to beat off fast

THE MATINEE I TOOK CHICKEN IN

I want to hold your hand just hell of it

a hundred and one famous shells a field of male space

a projection of outside rinsed with breeze

that there is no escaping from the now here

so I should feel famous you are telling me because a celebrity

scores so many creative types in New York City

eavesdropping on a reaffirming bankruptcy

you are just covered in pearls from head to weary baby

earned exhaustion as social rod your weary smile

hit me all the way from Roebuck

I descend into a hole of coal-black

wherein I dig a spanking fool's gold

hotel suite of memory I display my confidence various

put in letters to you double you triple too

what kind music caring scientifically molds your mood

I have brushed so mint me make me limited too

you can dance that is when tempos alter light

and ships land the buildings being cleaned they are aglow

you have drunk you have smashed every last plate glass it was a false fire

OCCUPY STREET

no worse than making fakes
apples redder fall
with plump would-be pimps
unstable at their posts remarking
neighborhood characters in pitch
blue to shape a chart of distant streaks
riffs coast out of two bars
and collide throwing night upon the floor
where a bit of glow goes to say
you are known on Facebook, elsewhere in
a laptop on a laptop you don't own
your staggering compulsory dance fits
to a beat of growing grass leaves
strong enough to crease asphalt
near dank stations alert
on a watchlist to which preservationists beat
their drums their tambourines afire
an asterisk so glaring sunny
no one reads the fine print
whipping past at the rump
of an on-demand wind-down
so you can toss another couple
into the dusty goldfish bowl of earbuds I am
wanting a miasma of nostalgia I am
wanting to touch I am
wanting to both touch and look
so very sorry for myself and you too
know this is my name
spend fewer words on your shirt
I call a muster of passersby getting away
from myself almost free whiskey
neat and brown as my wife's hair

ONE OF THESE GIRLS

one of these girls called after a state
prospectors stripped bare
to lots of cans concrete shops like dice
you pick up or she picked another one
to lift a cool glass slab
no voice meets your ear you hear
serial digital numbers kiss like
again a sampler hit like horse
prophylactic bonbons see her sack hum
now glow where one of these girls
knows her state song her bird her stone
flower pale this warming weather
wind forlorn bachelor sixty-one was it
sixty-seven I'm not him
here to hear this chorale or
she is not here for you this night
she ate night its gaps her dirt pie
will you fertility stumble
the team make a stake miss salty
cake asleep in type foundry
downy cheek to tapestry spread
you grasped at a pull tab
as if that were some kind
arrowhead they splashed
lead there too
so clean it out wash it off
that curb or this curb or stop
tulips fly apart in noon
and something is decomposed to fly
invisibly you study how
to slot your fingers in airports
precipitate of lemonade ash

tried on boys pants and fits those belts
you count yourself in or no
to dance with five four partners to platters
flame aristocracy's last pretense slash
worried new smile back from Berlin come
sooner consumer put down your cart
America's atonal dissident talents
heavy no nodding to drone guitar
just there on your belly
never nicer you little miner
pass the salt
some of these girls draw
on more than one account
that she was there monsoon purple
or blank as a temp beneath fluorescent stars
spank in nervous puddle
public do I still do I
figure as a fugue in your life when moons
break in your loft
reminding dandy professors of Shakespeare
who knew one of these girls
not a spider or minor
she is of a set to be
a victory faster

EVERYTHING IS GOING TO

As we unlocked it
there was nothing
in the safe
I wanted
to embrace
someone there
so intent to record
all we saw
paying attention meant
forgetting
everyone
but you
sexy
at that age or later on
a kind of stage
your solitude
a fictive situation
parceled among the crowd
multiplying your every gesture
in outline
unto degradation
I wanted to stop
defending comfort
and touch you to
begin undoing
the rigmarole
of our passing
union

GRANDMOTHER SNUFF

Born to be. Under amplified sermons cliffs erode. All this they wrote
out and folded before leaving. Out at collar, they arrive bringing collars.
To collar. If I knew who they were, I would let on. Give forth. Sunrooms
awaken the home. Summer afternoons grant a lemony pucker we share
evenings. Care, careless one. We do care and they do. Paradox nurses
workers. Then the others they were. Clean tools, sharp now, in orderly
files. All this sad on ice, when in a cooler. Unopened, Hank lies sober.
Uneasy to read his flat lip, or just leave it. Forever and now. See a snake
pass across the trail. Trace mottoes scratched in clay. Inky. A bright gang
here. Freedom lights fuses. These my embarrassed words, embroidered.
Fly outward, menacing satellites so fragile. A strong headwind awakes
your familiar, the tattooed actor. What washes and rusts in the ocean,
you ask him, livid with unspent blame. Anger drips on the barbecue.
Meaning beefs. Calm as cows, you are so skittish with strangers, all right,
okay mystery. To own up to livestock. Your generation born in wards.

GRANDDADDY OLD GRAND DAD

In a pickle jar. Designed to grow molds. Green swims. Plastic kettles of
brine. On wheels without wheels within them. Small commands, so as
to drive through curtains. Stopped in traffic, what was bought behind, in
pocket a penciled envelope. To be lost in. Why all horns seem major, stuck
in a row. Just in key, in time. Make a citizen's arrest. Write a letter to the
editor. Themes close to the actor's heart. Kindly a greeter stopped me on
entry. Picture us misty where they removed the one-hour photo booth.
True story, or it could be. I will sup with Poseidon, or cry in my own soup.
An entertainment. Airs come in off the sea and pause, huffy, a whiling
time. Breezes such as fall to earth, as newsprint, smack in driveways.
We got used to these other days. In the back pages wars go on yet. Cut off.
Commanded forward. Based on projections. Moving fronts. Tendrils furled
in parlors. Inky. Wait for the mood to lift. No, lift it.

WIFE WELLBUTRIN

Out hanging balloons to mark the way, I vary colors, firecracker by
milk, then yellow fire again. At last the night party, no money in that
inkwell, different every yesterday. The picturesque avoided as fenced.
Bridge another arc in dark; cross a real metal bridge. She walks alongside,
before or behind. Sometimes these rushing places. Now she leads.
We grip our bags firmly beside ourselves. Salt air bursts each thought
bubble. Sweeps us into night on the out breath. All roads lie scattered
with alarm clocks' gutsy guts. Gleam as they bleep. Only one mote counts
at a time. Watching the rushes. Not seeing what is so reassuring, the *shh* of
rain on skylights. Yet it is still. Come listen. Soft-spoken workers arrive to
sweep the chimney though we haven't one. Another ant trap will go missing.

FATHER WORK

Oracular always, the summer sun rolls its arcs. Read shadow scripts you
forget what went unsaid, the significant look. All that milk spilt over
nothing. Leaves a lot. Of course where you haven't been is there the while.
Too much imponderable detail nevertheless graces. Try to think it, not
only of it, nor yet through it. Each character unwinding a waxy scroll, from
this time to another. If they break. Sometimes you wait for a story, then
listen as the illustrated familiar auditions in his strange tongues. Farm out
a decade's empties for sea glass. Another collection goes uncatalogued.
Or emblazon her every change of expression. New gospels swell where the
dusk glows. Turn calendars ahead a year, not a day too soon. Hear all those
bottles clank colors in shallows, or could be some waterfowl. Hard to tell.
Hidden, a line of sand heaps up, cursive, fixed for breath.

MISTRESS DAMAGE

Blue light is special. Hesitate to take the moonlit stroll. Because animals. Fenceposts. A silver car, not a squad car, patrols. Only seems to be, not means to be, here and there, coming to and going fro. Say we are juggling and you watch all the pins. Or each. Or throw in one or another. Eventually all walks are circular. Stitch me that. A lot of good correctly described as home. Framed, there to ponder. Say more. A child couldn't believe we were each and all blameworthy. Then all homes are moving. Though one's own is enough, and each loved. Of course uncalculated watercourses unform part of the turning earth. Really. Stereo songs celebrate or chide what there is to squander. If I had a turntable. Night's Braille moo calls that bluff.

CHOIRBOY SKITTLES

Rain days grasses bristle under and shine. Water steps across and down, over and through. Leaves it shakes as it goes. And those others, they keep comfort. A cone of combustion zips up, unzips the storm. We are set to awake unalarmed. Gone down to the park, you see deer look up from dandelions by the fence. What you lack in breakfast you make up for in strange graffiti lore. The sum of initials in a heart may be a tree overgrown with ivy and oaths. Anyone can play the recorder. It is not an order.

COUSIN POT

A band snaps aloud. Piles and piles of speakers. A parade striking soon.
You hear it gather behind stores, their fronts blue and steel. Sighs hesitate
up a dim hotel hall. Then you are outside. I'm afraid the establishment is
out of clay pigeons. We forgot so many favorites, still there is nothing to
fear. A species of faith. Seeing Uncle Sam's finger wag, close your eyes,
type by touch. Why not begin listing trees. Aspen, birch, cherry, dogwood.
Winsome is a word goes unspoken. Pert, puzzle, inquire. Faster as some
cycle without spokes. Low to the ground. A job done. Against riotous
skies the town stands down. Puzzle a verb. What was interrupted, put
down, now is rooted. Recorded under bylines. Scarcities gather. Yesterday's
magazines dry as flour.

FRIEND'S GIRLFRIEND KOOLS

Part of outside slips in with August's traffic. It shows where clothes need minding. Here are many gardens. A truck gleams its fine details at noon. Maybe airbrushed. Like the side of a black can in green caffeine colors, lizard tongues, snake curls, neon flame. Jealousy in emulation, pride in restraint. The hallowed pump rightly foreign. Yet in its place. A new-made strange shed. An old shed strange. Stores a space we duck our heads there. Call that a species of nodding. Another carbon drawing brings up changes as we turn toward it. As if sunflowers. As if we could walk into the display. Screen doors need saving, stitch with floss, accept perspective. Borrow a pencil. Because before long. Lines of parents nodding. Not in approval or estimation or judgment. Keeping time. Speaking in hushed tones, these are awake.

SISTER CHABLIS

Change colors until your jacket's out at sleeves. Fold it for another town's seasons. The escaped almanac says October will ignite some days, weave its mulch, come down as a torn quilt. This almanac with dates scratched out, useful still. Ghosts just are their clothes. Certain planets, beady-eyed, elliptical, tuck in as for second supper. Heavens their table. Do not forgive all that I say, but choose. A setting or outer atmosphere. Some ways the land lies please. Or it is cussed hardheadedness. We jump feet-first into rivulets. Only a little. It hurts. When the rooster crows, alone you toss and turn. The bag man, says the inky actor in voiceover. As if that made sense, dawn clears the counters.

MOTHER OLD FASHIONED

Past parti-colored grasses at field's edge, a bright tin can dangles cut twine.
We did leave by this road. Herds startle, because they will. You were telling
me potluck secrets, and now that I have forgotten them, your photo is
in Mexico. Steam in the ears may make for better hearing, years later.
But how about that. One day. There is one day always. Mix it, and let it
precipitate in you.

BROTHER OXYCONTIN

My brother isn't here. I wake and know. But you are, and somewhere he
is, somewhere else. Sudden violence in father's snores and when they
stop. A few thoughts like drum-cracks. Let them be. A deal was struck,
hand under thigh. Who was blind, who made a bad bargain, who fed
the famished. We were to arrive at a mountain. Neither of us a candidate
for apotheosis. Shot on the sidewalk, in a snapshot, phrases written on
our backs. Then they still use red pencils. That mountain, undermined by
shafts of fool's gold, was never ours. Yet we never wanted it. The minutes
of the mining company listing all they paid in meal. My brother went to
make peace with an oligarch, goes by Dusty McScrooge. I was for joining
miles of gentle dispute to a big city. So I thought. We became weavers just
itching for the times. Then all lines went down. A humming arrived, a long
electric echo. You are forever standing outside stores. Tell me where we
meet tonight.

NEW OIL TODAY'S MEN

She wears genuine out yells
at wrappers that line wood-
land trails low down circle
round the moon her index
rings spoiled skies hang
a while filthy cummerbund and tie
hands pick the looming white
will to blow Pentagons bigger
opening weekends crowds
automatic pants roll down downy
make greasy leg holes oilier
showing pressing fibers gold white
essence of what is not not known
Megadeth T-shirt poetry Spoon
T-shirt poetry spleen greeting
rakes after the last hand folds
on the last smooth hopeful lap
take all holistic perfumes
every homily baked fresh this day
skip to my drill or private will
I make your life a living hell
clamber up the sodden steps
with mallets on pallets
let jewels shine free forever

STOP ME BEFORE

The turnout is smaller and smaller
wanted charismatic leaders set in firms
if I kill again the jungle surrounds us no
consolation where record stores used to be
last fifty pages outlaw bible blank
watching squirrels is total magic
making posters in orange and pink on a Mac
we made these books by hand we stitched them
you are late for brunch I want to kill again
if our chairs were more comfortable if
servers on skates heaped popcorn stout
if an oak splits apart in laughter in that
splitting its sides it could feel emotion
you know what I give up if plants had feelings
they do not so shut up shut up shut up
I think I will walk home but take the train
every old man on the planet burns with lust
some tween wants me to see she hates her dad
how she tilts at me the diary rolling off her Bic
she could kill me with her pen in an electric chair
matrons in the midst of fantasy series too easy
try to dry my face in a towel full of yesterday
uncertain project man these texts I smoke on stage
I hate the word craft call me

FICHTE

I sit on propositions what will
disperse clouds watermelon green
drop me again into your trap hurt me
it all comes from goes back to
fossils you hear a kind hand behind
rubbing your shoulder your thigh
not too hard just right ink stitch
cups a boob toward the table lamp
bubble cursive not really from girl
a fine period poster refolded
ants to apes see me it is in line
in order not alphabetized still pure
you call your truth hate and slay me
hit me with it baby till I babble curse
you're a high high croaker on the totem
generating style only for you is my curse
shoot up brain dust make me feel shade
it hurts living free and always having to die
I get on top and ruin another futon
while you're in the hall calling out heat
come back in with another outfit
crumble on my chin knock over the lamp again
it all makes sense to you there's no saying

PORCUPINE FEVER IS GONNA GET YOU

Look back no do not look back
I was beautiful in my younger days
every tire track a work of art
Mauritania Kenya had never seen such
I wrote the longest text and now
I can't send it from Mumbai India Gobi
what time is it there is no time for this
ugly palace stand sentinel over us
vacuum women wear orange headphones clean
all the shady lonely men you will meet
doors open close them soft though
sticky second-class car thighs sticky
think of dinner two Ugg prints on the moon
moans make pain sound good getting off
on it hurts this mess cats tykes
keeping one thousand calendars it's too much
it's so much a bookshelf from dead phones
an interview and a blog deal
just to dance after a day at desk
I can see why at moments but can't
make it happen really break the mold
so this could be an orgy of tears
everyone just holding each other's jewels
bawling about hurling the world in a bin
not enough ears for this urgent appeal
under the mic stand I'm wanking now
and whiskey makes me angry a mean mean drunk
I need Sue to be my life coach or you and she's fake
a calming chamomile infusion
placebo hugs make skin leathery or thin
I just slap more lotion on and forget the last hour
let me hear from you no words

I just like your moaning whatever the cause
spanked or fucked or confused or pleased
at harvest time I will look into your silent eyes
and we will find meaning in quiet
agreement that at last we know under the moon
how evil we are how calm and how true

FAGGOT SAID THE GUY IN THE TRUCK

I do not think I will ever suck
a poem as lovely as a dick
Loretta Buick said one night
taking me on her bike
down Lefferts Boulevard
I will ever remember
her Debbie Gibson T-shirt
fifty cities and towns
I'd only been to
the rain baby cocks driving cocks of rain
part dawn like Kirsten Dunst
part sunset like Virginie Ledoyen
rides no hands behind a tough
a woman more Arc than Joan
set me down on any curb
Sunset Park mutilated by gin
as in outer space no up no down
no number of dives
no number at all

WISHED FOR HATER SEQUEL

Burst of piano mash starts it
creasing general intention for indifferent brunch
gaggles of obvious friends some there
some not tilted to fresh reports the hospitals the schools
the formation of cliques without crystal structure
that shit could be called a crystal stayed behind a filter
waiter chided me for tossing salt over the wrong
talk about superfund superfun spots future grandparent
I signed your forearm with a fingertip you moved
back to my lap where my phone repeated my ex-wife's name
punters without butter or manners or mammaries
team sport headaches why you can't get off the bench
who wished she had the balls to brick a Starbucks
stop telling me telling me we should all be Shakers
did you see the bit in the tabloid what said
all human nipples will soon run dry

LOTTO BLUES

I cough dreams diamonds come
rooftops scenic places of which you recall
James Brown facts car chase easy search
hearts pump honey butter wiggle toes
KONY 1802 Stendhal was here
lucky delivery truck serial digits
since women do it better all day
shoot rims smack plate glass hard
a fight to the polish you have
such a dead smile it kills me

I WILL NOT BE EXPRESSED

I sense clean bones picked clean
flick noses at bars afterlife jazz
pipes and trombones come on in
this room is fine not near mint
throw the fight let the sea pull
under the waves your salt tears
taste seaweed rock you like waltzes
tinkle waste in a cup you're so pregnant
clocks spin lesser ballerinas
tops different dervish yelps
the exotic another erotic bore
learning to make pastries and laugh softly
a little too heavy for your mom's preference
walk away idle hours pool or no
did you know you knew ongoing siege
I need to make you tire into compromise
take you out and fuck with your dreams
the same but different I make an appearance
please please please let me let me let me
be insincere all night it's all right
I don't teach yoga haven't seen the regatta
I work the register of birds alighting
down stained platforms statues and curbs
today I know I will never teach yoga
but lick your ass truly call me you are lost

WELCOME MUSIC

Got dots and lines down there
walk around around like citizens
helmet legs to match pianolas
messages I distribute them you won't listen
what bleeds into an earth already vile
rude and disgustingly
you say I will always be hungry for perfume
wrestling damp sheets oily pillowcases
send money to agencies that follow
NSA CIA FBI NSC INTERPOL MI6
degrees prove degrees you're genius and so what
fairer than an orchid white as sperm whale ambergris
too hot for nerves galleries
swift I am at a boil at four a.m.
when will I spitball the concept of glamour
lust's busted trumpet
too new to be polished
let it rust

IF THERE BE A SEASON

Use paint glue scratch strip-
per poles permanently
time a new campaign
flip off real friends
keep pictures on detachable drives
litter under copter spots
beatbox cop talkie static
fudge peanut butter pains oh stains
be annoyed be fooled it is love but don't say it
propose projects willows
pack brown paths tubercular caves
use less yeast
set a dry cow pie afire
say yurt
meditate at vanity
be on the run just because
close eyes with your hands your own
have emotions you can't keep
larger cup holders
practice one way for a minute
stop it again tickle

BIG RED BOOSTER

Dusting the pantry nobody washed but all touched
chair where the man of the house sleeps fist-handed
traveled all his days so as never to save the Earth
suspended supermodel at his side actually a scholar of Proust
opium a La-Z-Boy predator joystick operator
needs to sleep like a tumor beside his woman
we don't need fields to fill the drug store only plants
uniform wings sweat socks
pixels slump Arizona sky never shows
hedges empty of natural birdsong
retired officer watch suburban streets fill with deer
the empty streets of my home town almost mute
the deer out of it at noon as if in one headlight

ALL YOU CAN

This is so good it's fucking disgusting I want
to eat these fries until I die of it just spooning
garlic aioli out of a rubber tub damn I like
the taste of your spunk your sperm your juices
down another taco I eat I'm going to burst
get me a tongue one with everything
and some rice to stick to my face like a girl
on a UNICEF coin box mid-eighties fucking ice cream
mainline ice cream with pickles and pork
mixed right into the scoop dirty pizza Halloween
slices like swallowing a row of crumpled ones
another helping of tartare tuna or steak
if I stop talking call 911 but if not let's hit
the meatball shop and BYO Bailey's
bags of coke buds that goddamn cake
at the wedding was insane let's order another
and never get married just have it for a week
let zits fester what may this is end times
I'll see your pot brownies and raise you
every variety of oyster at Prime Meats
dim sum tomorrows
wanting you wanting you never full
of wanting you wanting me wanting you
know I know you want I want to you know
I want you

FOREVER BACKPACKER

Leash me lead me to Miami
vinyl singer signs a lover waits for me
it gets heavier when we talk about wives
what we talk about is veins
funny come in stories where a stranger
injects romantic heroin
between sheets staining them
opium green nobody understands anything
they are baffled by dreamy fascination
but we think it's not a transaction after all
it's person person you know you're getting warm
we've crossed into slave
states French history French kissing
tongue wrestling triangle trade
crotch honey palm sugar simple syrup lip
sell it all at South of the Border
if you can find it and drag it back
and you can because I'm a boner with a rental
the motel room's distracting blaze
I wanna be your dog but a terrier room
perhaps a Great Dane Pit Bull service
strong dignified and dumb and proud of my pride
practicing lost national anthems under the breath
our Rough Guide so so out of date

THE GREAT-UNCLE DEAD

Poetry is the cruelest month
posters by thousands folded by machine
mild reminders to take note
of something harmless and bland
as sugar packets, restaurant mints are free
April, May, Tiffany, Annie
it's that time of the month
hand in your virgin efforts neatly typed
not the first you ever
but you can count on your fingers
would be hitting send even now
the lately dead the recently not with us
it is hard to rhyme dementia with
she was the sweetest woman
not training me all the time like mom
do you know what I mean by training
it can be the littlest thing
sometimes I was surprised a specialist even existed
like posture but with Gram I rode bareback
skied the steepest slope at Gstaad
she is so dead now probably rotten or rotting still
it's been almost a year she's not here
it's easier to love her now she's gone
remembering the strange Belgian candy
even her snuff habit seems cute
or well quirky she was from another time
she said she snorted cocaine in the fifties
and I believe her she looked so tiny
in that outsized diaper bikini by hotel pool Havana
the pictures she kept in a gold box
just fool's gold leaf on an ordinary wooden box

the oils and drawings were more demure
a bit off compared to the moldings
dust on the hard candy
once she tried to get me to shout delightedly German words
but I couldn't pick them up I mean that's not me
I'm as modern as they come
I sent Topher a pic of my pierced clit
just shaved and immediately regretted it
half of his school knows I have a ring
if they knew I took it out the next day
and the skin grew back I look at it and you can barely tell
it feels different still if you know what I mean
I don't think Gram would have done that
if she were my age, now, or maybe
she would have but she would have taken a real picture
and put it in her gold-leaf box and would never ever
have shown Topher with the lights on unless he was especially nice
and what's wrong with that nothing
what's wrong with being rich and overqualified
for the second-tier philanthropic society you chair
the best of everything my father said really shouting
the best of everything I'll give you
no one plays his hi-fi anymore
except me when I'm alone in the place
it's clean as anything Maria cares for
but you can tell the knobs are stiff
the platter creaks when you settle a record
we have everything Fleetwood Mac ever
including white label bootlegs
and all the Stevie Nicks solo
when I lie there I like to wear one of my father's hats

my feet on an ottoman
just singing don't blame it on me
blame it on my wild heart
Gram had a wild heart she did
some people thought she had a cold heart
and maybe that's true and it was a wild heart too

NO KEY TO THIS ONE, NO TUNE

falling slumped into grown bones hurt can't stop
stretching contacts thinner by night
a sour sound greeting jokes mimic of drum kit
to say you got it is to say not enough
make dance to postcard spill apple rebus
clean clean hardwood the cherry trim
stirs appetite but one knows no food gift
will go uninspected unjudged the wistful fool
scorned into the taller grasses or gazing grain
tripping macchiato at door next morn
don't knock rooms around and raise no dust
let it hide in the most positivist tomes
there there a little rain gets Irene higher
she seems to want a part I have
beyond good and bad actors a part is a part
hysterical rhythms lift tail ends of lines
she's not laughing not not laughing
so old but better to be mellow with a sting
go wash the floor more stories later
just drafts words blow here there
bowlike lips on my cock aghast tomorrow
her face so composed no one in the pub knew
a secret life long contemplated burns away just smoke
giving off a last puff of purple
what towels stack neatly in dust
what tattoo ink finally dries
dissolve to a far shore where money multiplies
and we are starving crawling living
like flies apparently open to warmth and dung
bring us drugs they do then they bring us food
the brain of the jukebox a little addled

complex person what emotions he hides
his orange face in green green eyeshade
douchey guys make clatter at the bar
a Taurus spills reggae at the curb
a schizophrenic college friend comes to mind
posting photo of an iris on Facebook not his own
someone Photoshopped the fuck out of that big blue eye
we're all wet with sweat and so is the most annoyed
girl pasty white hot and bored the world the end

HOW TO GET TO APRIL BLUE

enter gentle mantles varnish an apology
we're here we're orange falling engines bless the streets
just living for no one reason livid computable silent
digital wrist can't get off tiled steps
arcing paths of lives so storms can break
fast rocks and pop conference room garnish
projects launch with a sigh doing lines on a CD
these games I spy must tonight be fun it must
many will suffer and die do not know why
lens yourself for change you carry good curves
private joker say it out loud do a pole dance on the train
it takes forever to get an ice cream too heavy to carry
you just give up stranded foreign accents make pass
so you compose yourself against your face your lies you know
too well aluminum countertop pots stand on foreigners
youthful introspection just a slab of neck
a ruler to measure the poem for a prison frock
or a heavy bass guitar strap filigreed
moist moist moist moist moist vagina upside-down cake
make it white whiter correct bias darkly
trajectories in gulfs or suburbs for you
down down down down the red carpet stairs to the loo
pay by hand and get away through airport fast food
and white cube galleries the point if there ever were one
when it is right to cry during the camera interview
seemed to me the best reply blank paper

ROOF GARDEN HERITAGE SITE

brutal concrete struts
take us down
orphan's homes
sharing beds I think thinking you
you and you
woke later hungover fed clam cake
crowds know how you make it why be specific
bound to slither into dry carcasses
becoming no mummy but Braille nonsense
because you can't even grasp getting-around Braille
to teach us of outlying suburbs stores spots
finding no radiation curse leave it
feed servers' children nothing just steak tartare
or gather to loiter not talk grip cold gloves
you are a squeaky gate pretend you're Gertrude Stein
but thin and sexy will fuck anybody
as one season melts the street literally
it brings other purer kids to soft park
picture cleaners pouring cleansers in gutters
a few weedy lots what bounce in the wind
you stand at the fence a Camel in your pucker
wolf man poster rained straight into a timber pole
what is a serviceman a servicewoman
to the pure joy of hopped-up children
flinging overhead rags or plastic bags
it takes parks and muscles I suppose
to sit seeing patterns hardly random
hardly plain come closer sit near us
feeling wrung turn pixel knobs

AUTO-BRIGHTNESS

weather vanes piled by curbs
mirrored in café glass
gone scavenging noon
plastic witches I am wanting
cleavers left in the Halloween sky
my hands reach to house mother blue
effectively only in gesture
such trash as hits you
when yesterday's toxic fluid
your digital watch fades to
blank warm Casio again now the mute is on
dog pissed sidewalk come down
you bringing this neighborhood aura where you are
from where daylight taps cornices
dust on closed blinds where was
a law firm a campaign a psychic
turn toward country in any direction
to step directly into earth
stairs here go every way
apocalypse gets a sick day
files updated on a soap bubble's skin
calendar page objections roll
the down your neck back sticks
in my palm if you have time
in the clean quiet room a man said
keep doing this just this this
and that man was me
cover your love in pleasantries
ink up your back and the girl at the party had
an frightening cartoon killer there
it works like baseball or thinking of your aunt

gestures gaits to say surrender
hardly enough for solid
sleep or pants she and you are so hard
your teeth are so fragile
that you are easy

BUFFALO NICKEL, TOOTHBRUSH, CRUDE

hardly have I always worked fall
gymnasiums down tinier
townships eventually tears up
over underlip of Shirley boss
knew she was pulling clambering bodies
sweat rope damp mats energy drink
hung walls there to disappear
behind but still at center
hub puberty strife fuck my life
I own a share of lugubrious gropes
fade gray milk mulch what that bubble
blew its pop bought round this world
blaring terror I terrorize others
families languages nobody understands
suburban towns fade to digits
by baring all and terror I
go where memories go over into fear
the instant a head snaps
making way for adroit photonegative
Instagram settings saplings weeds
kernels seams are the common enemy
if the world is going to end
you come eat poison and it is
pills and preparations you take
I am talking about myself
in an empty room
when nobody's looking
listening to a seventies album
momentarily impossible to get right
chirping beetles helicopters rats
fields need be gone fallow

to fertilize even a ten-foot plot
without the smallest gift to science
let it go make yourself look cool
the last person afraid of the lens
I will be a spokesperson then
shoving shameful carts and eye charts
crispy snacks coasters and gin
late precarious learning you can't scratch
any other way is another short wait
for a ticketed dancer a big win
the next day finds you splashing blue
from a still pail
dumping some crude oil
on top of it to prove it
slotting in toothbrushes past prime
finer use for neon green
slot some loose change there
it is your coined coin

NEW MAKE

what comes next is
possible to theorize one
period emerging now
explore late ailments
see shells or pounds of ruler
also a lecture at Choate
spurred her ken for new
nests that break ice
got the germ of moribund style
what is it that Joe wants
to free poetry from
deliberate space of wail
conveys a need for hugs
one more future among none
not quite forgotten now
easy to get heated at a lectern
after drinking television looks
better be stumping for ease
that offspring will steal
like lovely stickers peeled
from white shapes that held
tells you she was born built
as much as born to slip
into a car driven by a diver
you and she do not yet
perceive as form critique allows
for just some laughter not waste
pretense unforgiven hidden patience
every tentative second awaiting buses
means you are wanted
like a wanted man is wanted
eyes deliberate blur past posters would I
lick off your lipstick and rouge

HOPSCOTCH SMUDGES

The day you left
Do not leave
I cried out why
Any unsolicited female
My heart froze numb
Advertising material
My mind blank as
On this property
It were baked Alaska
Newspapers and magazines only
Vanilla noggin rocking
No dogs allowed
You stuck kiss to my ear
Do not feed
As if caught in a conch
The sea will not make any more
Passionate whispers
Boring art
I locked those secrets by a slide
Security provided
Hung with ripped phone cords
Guardian solutions
Rippled abs
Long gone forever
We deliver
For you
To you
For you

GAME SHOW THEME MIX

Orange and violet chipped
Here and there milk might damp
The statue plastic stitched
To a steel pedestal with fire
Like flutes echoing lightning skies
A rat's ass and more this sudden person
Somebody who is somebody to nod
Where you belong
Flowers of fire
Potted Italian men solo loving
There is a way kinder position
Come late time plain flat
Moving with crew
Out on artificial lake
It's so sad to be alone
Slide a packet of nylons
Down the floor
Your floor

WORDS BY KARL MARX, TUXEDO BY RIOT

Inevitable as in England ancient Roman law
Opposite of the social
Complete and conscious return of man
With his good money after the overthrow
Of the whole conception of history
In practice lost all credit
An element of positive, profane
Painful imaginings
Guilty of this or that maximum loss
Transmitted from the past
Like a nightmare on the brain
Batters down all Chinese walls
According to age and sex
You are horrified
At our intending
Let us now take
Women screams
Most radical flare up
Of bourgeois claptrap
Sketch of the course
A precise study of strikes
Movement in abstract form
Is the genuine war on the situation
The artless ways of the child
Standard and model beyond
Silly lives of Catholic saints
All the other brave words
Behind which lurk
Efforts of mechanical genius
Glory brings
Organized like soldiers

A reasoned ardor
With the bad side
To be judged
Is it surprising in the final
Linen or silk
Men as flax
Closely bound up in sheaves
The hand mill gives you
All such phrases
Setting in motion arms and legs

THE BARN PARTY

No one came under
leaves drenching plastic

cups lit up over-
passes pissing thrills

a ragged border, call it Texan lace God
bless this memory hole

hot set top warm soaps
animals out race streets closed off

locked with shops
so they can paste new tip cup jokes

the first last days.

Prepare soups in the reference
section, painkiller

sting the singer, signs the Scorpion
traced on Hayden's smashed

lens flyers dream they mulched those
fields in turn turn turn your mop to

rented speakers, lights too
I believe you, saying I am going to

welcome shades of structures, plaints
pleats, ripped faces, subway walls, the will

got me here, so I made lists
and lost in the fall all invited

sought other reunions
studying to be yoga instructs

best coffee in town, Om, it must be
payday

GONNA DIG UP OZU

To place a grown woman
use tough gloves
in rock gardens
out front dust shows

depends on how you turn about home
whirl around sunset

slides of shoestring tours
U-turns, artifacts
stop talking for one second
time today

In the house
we eat chimes cut
flowers clouds of broccoli
on oilcloth

A blue light switched on
deep in me pits

Painting a peacock badly perched
on drooping vines
on yarrow weeds
on a placemat

Making little sense edible altogether
microphones we carry sponge
words like pages
or croutons, familiar, offline, dedicated

Epiphany telling this
I am not able to say I have quieted days faster

Getting on my last being's coil
recall where we were just
at start

A bit of rain in online trees
even stones take it in
these features in today's camera work

BARS AND LOUNGES ON YELP

Blood and tears marked as wet
ripped days, trash goods
sift use

For what colors blue colors orange colors green the field
(outdoors in)

rusting tracks melt stops in snapshot
polite smile for the time

few these days printed sneaking under a shelf
into the ward at nights that rain

the chase itself
of course along viaducts and suburban tracts
would have been
workers such as shrug the game never was

owning up to that patented trance
join an inflated parade baby effigy
tethered to a much-shot street

comfortable couches in there
ambient music
ends up on the share drive
the administrator named Boulevard

HARD DRIVE SCRUB

Now you're in
there is nothing you can't see can't you the

electric lights: bobbins
an energy, quantity, number this
eidolon or abstract thing violence at eight
point five million seconds per

organic bananas ninety-nine cents
a pound or several make babies
of us all of us

again data's voice so girlishly enacts
Archie Bunker accents
what's hidden in fat slacks power dons

then it is finally indescribable

open it mouth it bites it
humid climates and tins in bins
subtropical fairly spread
in air, part of the greater
circling and plunging, hover however
furling huge blooms fairy of death

I scarce know what
it is sharp and free
its present whiteness
it is charming notes
anonymous Swedish admirer
the joke is on

confess group facts fail
to say rejoicing Ssips
drinks ninety-nine cents
jump our bumps together baby
dumb friendship is best

ACROSS THE BOSS'S DESK

1.

                                       rub your glass

periscope dancer

that's there isn't

see here

                   there her

say it   rains musty crush

gold box flakes

                          say "sir" end under

leaves wet roofs a pension

locked-in tuna pen-

chant hello we getting tight

        I do not know you spooky person

                       just another real word
                       just ice for numb
                       rest perfect man
                       nurse woes
                       drop fans

down down well back a way we go

plinks on robot knee

who says I   don't have feelings
                        I have plenty

        me me

babble about
                    waterfalls
swim in
                    waterfalls

you are, like, a hurricane

one beard brags is
another straight   cut
our   ruler   torn

marking the limit
so seriously a few   inch

messes of lines
no need to write   a notice though
is it not beautiful when children do it

2.

set froze features to heat
stars moving means   they are   satellites of somewhere

adjusting the dust

        plug artificial firings

laptops in other zooms
        credits relax you are expecting
                sequences of circles
cant now reaches permanent bits
brightening sides of   buses
pressing pleasing   colors
        the glimpse we hear gather
massy smudges

sum it up for you
lots of nights lost

there is not a reason:
        not one single reason

this time being called forth
to be entitled and allowed

to travel the globe
never to pin
        just one little thought in any one head

jotting down costs
names hotels towns
brands   of milk

later what comes tumbling down
over lips in after years

3.

cut like a wedge into the cotillion punch, sour
swollen chin add freckles to that
examination in a glass the light alters
whole days could strand new saints

some joke about Poles
some girls in Poland
bright tape rewinding past magnetic Marguerites
making yourself up in an antiqued mirror

today another Stones show
plots dug in the street again dug in as in dug

a little more past where we two live

once more sad summer   is said   is said

to be a meaningful   shade
to coat   bricks

in blood printer's devil
pirate's booty dry mouth
Rough Guide to Las Vegas 2009
not your fault that
each sits in her way
painted fully

frame one in plastic bric-a-brac which way to be flexible
artists jamming
fish-infested seas

going to seed
in working bands
great-hearted men who meet the drink

4.

one popular adjective ushering
off a tenor

I've got something
speech speech

dial-a-movie
ringing again

and after climax of
whanging harem hammers

hammering on
the neighbor's baby grand
        a mad cry of freedom

5.

where the cobbler stops we raise our cups

rough grain gets on allover
lumber about crazed
foam bells starting to break

a startling question
remember about lemmings
the new girl's smock poses

                                        her sorrowful eyes
we each can't fit in a period
silently barkeep
kick us out into tonight

still spaces to litter with crushed shells

homeless persons or if you prefer hermits

T. S. Eliot might watercolor
Sundays all his life though in peanut colors

his greatest maxim:
keep it to yourself

6.

spar for prose
seeing us trellised
in thorny stereo no
        roses guns
shh this is uplifting objects
you can move things
just by thinking hello stuff stuff

today I will share
happy to be here happy to be there

someone read the minutes

all answer it's hard
these choice choices scrambled

emoticon victim you

me too, dizzy:

                    not to show it

spinning more, keep on turning
ditto machine purple
ditto ditto ditto ditto
ditto ditto ditto ditto

7.

it took authority to write it down
a committee to make it into a pile
and maintenance to screw the plaque to the wall

the exam samples are you afraid

when building sets for Polanski

open the guide for in-flight TV
so your thumb lies on *Ben Hur*

8.

linens and things

                    things and linens

where does it end

the most beautiful birdsong I've heard

continues when lightbulbs come on

I read your blog

this morning you call our role

a spaghetti western dish

wiping ointments discreetly in train cars

can you just pick this up and turn it on
learning separated by equals signs

wanting a new engine
black letter the word caboose

9.

he here who is poorer than Richard
down to the wire marathon

keep us breathing
windows
to tell less what we see through than why

this act of shredding pretending to be
illustrated step by step
figure one: jambs and knobs

now there gates there gates now
whisper the air melody air the whisper
couldn't you couldn't
you try to explain to try you

drink it all up
fall down in the muck
look at the leafy there
ascertain its color and walk away

classified men

tell you this our
nothing else rodeo

10.

getting references starts to get even
mister manners so at home
think importunate look-up
glimpse calm in the iris
just ice can you lick it
better digest the room twice wanting

a do-over liking your air
terrible with money flinch
could it you be friend to the end friend me one credit
please thank you come again oh please

11.

more prosy Saturdays flipping off the calendar
winging away into the wind
characters get older
font dry as the steward's eye

pure corn trashed
pure corn fuel scheme
pure corn oiled guns
pure corn hatred nut
pure corn sunset tongue
pure corn pet spider
pure corn bland wash
pure corn tattoo shop
pure corn inspected ham
pure corn sashimi
pure corn convention event
pure corn tortilla

12.

listen to tumblers here now
feel the safeness get up close

lift grain-colored highballs face
trouble puddles well in corneas' guts

oh disapproval palms
hearts can't eat out on this date

could this place serve what we need
if we knew what we needed

this review was funny three helpful two
obnoxious one, pass the gavel

put a hotel on the boardwalk
and a cap on the baloney bellboy

13.

once on this train why would I get off
really not knowing anything

breathing through a tube

fierce ruth after seven-elevens go dark

danger boys retire all smokes

when to my confessions booths slam shut no

matter too rough till morning test stop
the emergency reggae broadcast system stop

sleeping strange couches smell of man
how I remember grad school

would you call your mother a mutt
your country yeah just once in a long while

a cocky bastard voice in the skull
make me a man signing words not indifferent

clasp hands you couldn't make us
singing when the shower stops

PURPLE SNOW PURPLE SNOW

Come on now, talk
When they pull out on the breeze
There's no survivors
it's the simple stuff I need
how sweet romance is glum
The sad talk laws are broken on a hilltop
I'll take my chances with impunity impunity
Got you up And I could really give a fuck
Can't you stuff me?
So bad, so bad, so so bad so so bad
I remember lying, I don't remember a line
This is the city life—Hey lady, what do you need?
you're the kind of girl I never wanna make
Keep you in sight, Three of us is enough
Every night Dreaming, dream, dream it got stuck
But I won't pay the rent My little trick
Advocating a bottle of white I like you
say goodnight screwin' your graceful tongue
Stuff me that word I love your tinted eyes
I've got to melt it show me Take it neighbor
if my walkman fades keep my anthem
because the sun will melt the pigs, the fuzz, the cops, the heat
Because there's forty different shades of black
they don't need you anymore, little girl, boy, girl, boy
Because you feel that you're social
Don't even snow Don't even snow
Ya, Ya, Ya, Ya, Ya
quarantine the past 'Cause we need secrets
Because I'm rushing to feel this amusing era
you're empty and what did you expect?
I'd like to invite you to a taste of my chalice

this crime it is never complete
slow, sick, sucking scene full of punks
Can't you see the stuff I need?
If I could Then I would If I could
settle down settle down settle down
I need to snort up their drugs sleep it off
come and bleed with me Well, I got absolutely no one
no hands Nothing more than me
check out your public protests
Call and response, negative hope
remind you remind you
you got to take it Silent Can't you see?
There's no survivors School's out I need release
yeah baby oooh So drunk And I need favors
I'm taking everything the turnstiles
the courthouse's double-breast
the practice room the rose-covered floats the tokens and stamps
the Smashing Pumpkins the sharks their Vespas the plane
the pulse the traffic the road the drumstick the cinema stars
the fake oil-burning lamps the lines, open shutters, and the leaves
the war the city the grapevine the top of the Shasta Gulch
the hills of Beverly the horses and break-up divorces
the bottom of the Tahoe Lake the gum smacks the face the picture
the plane down the plane down the plane down
the driver the jam kids the ground the looks
the dance faction the plane down the plane down the plane down
the rock and roll era The street the queen of a canceled Pasadena
the foothills of my pride Let me sleep it off I need to sleep
I need to sleep I need to sleep I need to sleep I need to sleep
I need to sleep I need to sleep
I need to sleep I need to sleep I need to sleep

I would hope you see her face survivors
There are no spikes and plugs on their faces
Stone Temple Pilots Dad they broke me, dad, they broke me
Their throats are filled with the slow, sick, sucking part of me
sand waste concrete wedding rings psychedelic credit
Pull out their plugs Hit the plane down
Hit the plane down Hit the plane down
No one but myself to blame Chewin' myself with my hand
Hand me your pawn shop home arks Jasper's skinny arms
grandmother's advice a milligram up my sleeve
it's the way I'm living, right or wrong it's straight and narrow
Back right now I know you don't have wings
tie me up I deserve absolutely nothing they will agree
I need a in the elegant boats Then I would settle down
when I suck in kisses, it's ours and she won't let me break you out
That's what they made my hero say
She won't let you know that I need a right to touch her
'Cause it's secret cret cret cret cret cret cret cret cret cret cret
is it a crisis or a boring change why won't you let me?
Hey, you gotta pay I'm taking over the scene
I've Got you all up my sleeve
snort it up or shoot it down
You're never going to feel free
I'm taking over your life
asked nicely I don't have no function
You've done me favors 'cause I'm your neighbor
Hit down I buried you bachelors Hit the plane down
just humming my skateboard the night
It's a special one, it's made of gold
Back right now Lost in deltas and rivers
Down in Santa Rosa and over the bay across to LA

After the glow, the scene, I've been wasted for the last word
Well you greet Underneath shame about your family
Fly fly fly fly fly fly fly
My my my my my my my
Nature When cut it free Last words come up
ignored soul Go back to Heaven dream, dream
Never believe in what you wanna do
Did you say I know everybody wants to put you down
Write it on a postcard Because I'm rushing to feel you
It's a brand new era but it came too late
You film hack, I don't use your fade
in the August sun in the falling rain
but there's one thing I'll never forget
I don't remember a word but I don't care
I care, I really don't care
and they're coming to the chorus now
got you up got you up got you up got you up
Hit the plane down Hit the plane down Hit the plane down
there's no survivors
there's no survivors
there's no survivors
there's no survivors
there's no survivors
there's no survivors
there's no survivors
there's no survivors
there's no survivors
there's no survivors
there's no survivors

BLACK STEEL

(thing)	(thing)	(thing)	(thing)
(thing)	(thing)	(thing)	(thing)
(thing)	(thing)	(thing)	(thing)
(thing)	(thing)	(thing)	(thing)
(thing)	(thing)	(thing)	(thing)
(thing)	(thing)	(thing)	(thing)
(thing)	(thing)	(thing)	(thing)
(thing)	(thing)	(thing)	(thing)
(thing)	(thing)	(thing)	(thing)
(thing)	(thing)	(thing)	(thing)
(thing)	(thing)	(thing)	(thing)

SONGS FOR A COUNTRY DRIVE

1.

reach for a passenger side handle
the forest it stops it now
out of car morrow marked on drained device
to stay Tuesday roll in back
seat all knotted shirts

from plants that billow
and embellish the trail's
rest area tale of diet cola warnings
warming skin within

her argument sudden but not understanding it
whispers false show sawdust seen
tracked upon arrival in country
house memory goes below river party talk

an original pair on wheels
they like each other are like
spreading fluids over them
selves attractive so to
sing to move
all guests
gone

2.

this in site of a great thinker's homestead too
worried by work to picnic they find a visor left
stitched neatly with palm trees and the name
of a holiday town mostly rubbed

out with use
shining it brown yellows break through rainbows
the acrylic piping

nobody went near
empty trash buckets
there where the visor fell

why they that stopped before couldn't bend

bound to an acceptable ever-present position
some stranger on the web forgave you
for give up fighting cause

the state was not after all in any way
a grand scheme of things
it was nowhere to be forgotten

3.

away the light fuses keeps on
the road faces dangling
swinging censor-
ed digital memory method
so the viewer can't say who was

there only when standing
a round of water
stories not over asked for
complicated maps clubs conspire
for getting an escaped youth

victim of a new century of
slapping sense into prophets
that afternoon in the park corner the man was just dripping
footnotes in proper style

have the floor to dance four more
color strikes flashes
cymbals collapsing into nothing vitals

like speeding out of tunnels
as the rationale for mountain
network collapse stops making the news

4.

whose voice the commodore doubled back
little charmer in pajamas chewing wildflowers snapped
in hidden uncle's visiting lens
tumbler cradled in hitch of tennis elbow

so to be turned out from what mending
time and the elements precipitate in

a ride inside whatever winds throw
for stinging stretches never to know

you would not once put your finger on that string of

desert highway given to sad sacks making an ass
of what got many this far

hysterically dour
a fortunate error
now wanting doubts as to
how it sounds outside one long gone head

5.

so hot piece of far to go
blue then mixed then
voices in the car aren't ours

so much can be done in
a studio it takes the entirety of outer space to absorb

when he put his face in the vase
crying crayon on the walls
not seen every day
to think it is enough
to press buttons

to know where people come from
in rooms in Brazil you

read what the caption says
and who would you be to guess

otherwise pull
the safety blanket
over your head and say some
smart words about
the last ten books you read

6.

to be perfectly clear it means smiles
impossible raindrops keep falling into
eyes listing for the pause before applause
staring at atmospheres heavy like tons of

bricks clicking down around you auditor yon auditor you
remember when she said this feeling like home
wireless light become orange
and there was hearing again and again and listening

going out and getting on
the subway
out to the end of the line

to go down to where the ships would get
wet if there are ships and I've been told if there is a riptide
you let it take you
out and then on
a diagonal you
swim back